D1276922

How To Convince Your Parents You Can...

Care For A
Pet Sugar Glider

Amie Jane Leavitt

Mitchell Lane

P.O. Box 196
Hockessin, Delaware 19707
Visit us on the web: www.mitchelllane.com
Comments? email us: mitchelllane@mitchelllane.com

Mitchell Lane
PUBLISHERS

Printing   1   2   3   4   5   6   7   8   9

A Robbie Reader/How to Convince Your Parents You Can...

Library of Congress Cataloging-in-Publication Data
Leavitt, Amie Jane.
  Care for a pet sugar glider / by Amie Jane Leavitt.
      p. cm. — (A Robbie reader. How to convince your parents you can...)
  Includes bibliographical references and index.
  ISBN 978-1-58415-800-4 (library bound)
  1. Sugar gliders as pets—Juvenile literature. I. Title.
  SF459.S83L43 2010
  636.92'3—dc22
                                                                    2009001112

ABOUT THE AUTHOR: Amie Jane Leavitt is an accomplished author and photographer. She graduated from Brigham Young University as an education major and has since taught all subjects and grade levels in both private and public schools. She is an adventurer who loves to travel the globe in search of interesting story ideas and beautiful places to capture on film. She has written dozens of books for young readers including four others for Mitchell Lane in this series: *How to Convince Your Parents You Can Care for a Pet Mouse, Tarantula, Chimpanzee,* and *Chinchilla.* Amie believes that all living things should be treated with respect and dignity. She hopes that young readers will gain an appreciation for animals from all parts of the world after reading these books.

PUBLISHER'S NOTE: The facts on which this story is based have been thoroughly researched. While every possible effort has been made to ensure accuracy, the publisher will not assume liability for damages caused by inaccuracies in the data, and makes no warranty on the accuracy of the information contained herein.
    Special thanks to Eddie at GliderCentral for all his help with this book, and to the parents and photographers of the sugar gliders in this book for letting us use their pictures.

TABLE OF CONTENTS

Words in **bold** type can be found in the glossary.

In the wild, sugar gliders live in trees. This keeps them safe from predators. Gliders get their name from the fact that they don't walk around on the ground. To move from place to place, they climb, then glide. They can glide up to 150 feet—about half the length of a football field.

Chapter One

A PET THAT CLIMBS AND GLIDES

Many kids have pets. Some have cats. Others have dogs. You might want to own a pet that is more **unique** (yoo-NEEK). If so, you might consider getting a sugar glider.

This animal is tiny. It weighs only 4 ounces as an adult. It likes to snuggle into tight spaces (like your pocket). It has silky soft fur similar to the fur of a **chinchilla**. It has a bushy tail that resembles a squirrel's. It carries its babies around in its pouch—just like a kangaroo—and can actually hop off a perch, like a tree branch or even your arm, and glide around the room.

Sugar gliders sleep during the day. That's great news if you're a school-age kid, because while you're studying your fractions in math class, your pet is snoozing. When you get home, your pet will be all rested and ready to play with you.

Sugar gliders bond with humans by getting used to their smell. You probably don't realize that you have a specific smell, but you do, and sugar gliders can sense it. Once your pets know you, they'll want to climb all over you every chance they get!

Some sugar glider owners like to dress up their pets. This owner made a tiny hat for his suggie.

However, just because an animal sounds cute and looks cute doesn't mean it is the right pet for you. It also doesn't mean that your parents will agree to let you have one. This book was written to give you all the information you need to know about owning a sugar glider. That

fun FACTS

It costs at least $150 to buy a sugar glider. However, if you want a suggie that is spotted or a unique color, you could spend between $700 and $2,000.

way, if you decide you want one, you'll be able to explain to your parents why this animal would be a good pet for you and your family.

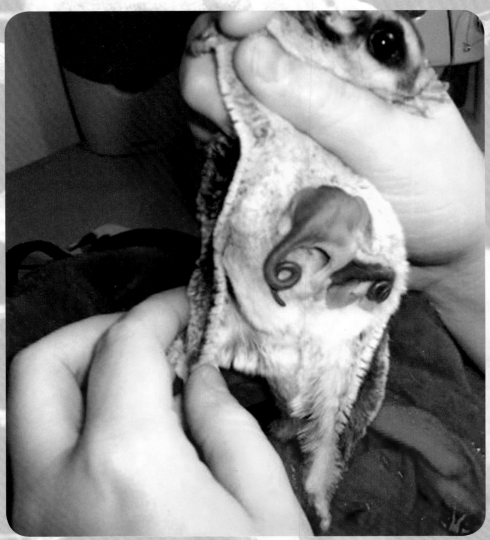

Momma Aspen shows off her pouch-riding twins. Baby suggies are born tiny, just like kangaroos. Their mothers carry them around in a special pouch on their stomach until they're big enough to glide on their own.

Chapter Two

POUCHED MAMMALS FROM THE LAND DOWN UNDER

Sugar gliders are mammals just like cats, dogs, and even humans. Hair covers their body. They have lungs. The mothers feed their babies milk. Yet sugar gliders are different from many other mammals. The females have a pouch on their stomach just like kangaroos, **wombats**, and **opossums**. Mammals with pouches are in a group called **marsupials** (mar-SOO-pee-uls).

Sugar gliders are also like kangaroos and wombats because they are native to Australia—a country known as the Land Down Under. Sugar gliders are also native to Indonesia, an island nation just northwest of Australia.

Some marsupials live on the ground; others live in trees. In the wild, sugar gliders rarely walk on the ground. That's because many larger meat-eating animals—such as snakes, **quolls**, and **monitors**— would love to eat them! When sugar gliders want to move from tree to tree, they glide to get there.

Gliding is different from flying. When an animal flies, it moves its wings up and down to lift itself into the air. Sugar gliders do not have wings. Instead, they have a piece of skin on both sides of their body called a **patagium** (pah-TAY-jee-um). This skin is connected to their wrists and ankles. When sugar gliders glide, the patagium acts like a parachute. Air pushes up into

"It's a bird, it's a plane, it's Super Glider!" The sugar glider's patagium acts just like a parachute. When its patagium is stretched tight, the suggie can glide around the room.

it, allowing the sugar glider to soar like a paper airplane.

A sugar glider is approximately 12 inches long: 6 inches is its body and 6 inches is its tail. Sugar gliders generally have gray fur and a black stripe painted between their eyes and down the center of their back and tail.

funFACTS

Wild sugar gliders live in colonies. There are usually 20 to 40 members, and two males father most of the babies.

Since sugar gliders are **nocturnal** (nok-TUR-nul), they have big eyes. This lets them see far away in very little light—perfect for an animal that hunts for food at night. They can spy a moth or other insect flying dozens of feet away and swoop down to snatch it up!

Sugar gliders love eating the sap from **eucalyptus** (yoo-kuh-LIP-tus) trees. They use their sharp nails to scratch off the bark, then lick the sweet liquid underneath. It's kind of like sipping sticky maple syrup. In fact, sugar gliders received their name because of their love of this tree "sugar." They also eat insects, flowers, and fruit.

Female sugar gliders usually start having babies at around nine months old. They can have up to three litters of babies per year. Each litter usually has two babies, or joeys. Sometimes a mother will have three or four babies, but that is very rare.

After a male and female mate, it takes only 16 days for the joeys to be born. At birth, the joeys are the size of an uncooked piece of rice. They are also blind, deaf, and pink, since they have no fur yet. The joeys have to journey across the mother's stomach and slide down into her pouch. They will stay there for about 10 weeks, drinking their mother's milk and growing. They double their size in about 14 days. By 40 to 50 days, they're about the size of a peanut. By the time they're ready to come out of the pouch (about 60 to 70 days), the joeys are the size of an adult human's thumb.

Sugar gliders are a little unusual because both the mother and father care for their young. They make very good parents. When they hear their babies crying, they run right to them. Both

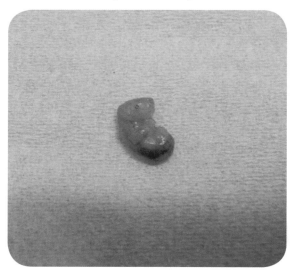

Sugar gliders are teeny-tiny when they're born. They're only about the size of a rice grain and weigh just 0.2 grams.

"It's tiring being cute." Once the suggies spend 60 to 70 days inside the pouch, they're ready to come out into the world. Young gliders are so small they can fit inside the palm of a person's hand.

parents also take the babies for rides on their back before they learn how to glide. The fathers teach them how to eat insects and other solid food.

In the wild, sugar gliders live only 4 or 5 years. Pet sugar gliders—or suggies, as their owners call them—can live for much longer. If people take care of their pet, a sugar glider can live for as long as 15 years!

There are many different types of cages that you can use for a sugar glider, but these Australian animals are happiest when their cage looks like the Land Down Under. Fill it with plenty of leafy branches for climbing, and cozy hammocks for sleeping. You can hang a shower curtain around the cage to keep their mess inside.

Chapter Three

CHOOSING A SUGGIE—OR TWO . . .

Many suggie owners recommend buying from a breeder instead of a pet store. Pet stores can be great places with lots of fun animals to see, but sugar gliders at pet stores have likely been handled by a lot of people. Because of this, they often have more diseases than animals sold by a breeder. Another drawback is that pet store staff may not know about everything a sugar glider needs to stay healthy. Breeders, on the other hand, raise their animals from birth. They know how to care for them. Thus, your chances of getting a healthy pet are greater if you buy from a breeder.

Wherever you decide to go, look around the place before you buy and ask yourself these questions: Are the cages clean? Do the animals seem happy? Do they have bright eyes and fluffy tails? Are their nails neatly trimmed? Are the animals quiet when you approach their cages, or do they make loud noises and

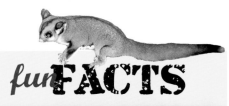
fun**FACTS**

Some people say that the "crabbing" sound that sugar gliders make sounds like an electric pencil sharpener or an electric can opener.

act afraid of humans? The answers will help you choose a healthy pet.

You can buy adult or baby gliders. If you get a baby, it should be at least 12 to 16 weeks old. By this age, the glider can live on its own, away from its parents. A benefit of getting an adult glider is that it will likely be familiar with humans. There are more adult gliders that need a home. You might want to adopt one from a **rescue**.

Since sugar gliders are meant to live in large groups, many people buy at least two sugar gliders. It's best to get two males OR two females. If you get a male and a female, make sure the male has been **neutered**. This is an operation that prevents the male from becoming a father.

Some people think that since a sugar glider is small, it can just live in a bird or rabbit cage. This isn't true. Sugar gliders need plenty of space to move around. The smallest cage you should get is two feet tall, two feet wide, and two feet long. If you get more than one glider, your cage must be larger than that. It's okay to buy a plastic cage or one made out

Just like kids, gliders love to play. These two suggies are chasing each other inside a Wodent™ wheel.

of non-rusting wire. Other types of metal can make sugar gliders sick.

Sugar gliders love to play, so you'll need to buy them a lot of toys. The most important toy to buy is a wheel. Suggies love Wodent™ wheels and Stealth™ wheels. They also like playing with kid toys. As a rule of thumb, anything that is safe for a child who is two years old or younger is safe for a sugar glider.

You should also attach some tree branches to the inside of the cage. This will help your suggie feel like it's living in the wild. You also need to buy containers for water and food. A water bottle can be wired to the outside of the cage. Inside, you'll need three food containers: one for wet food, one for dry food, and one for mealworms.

Since sugar gliders sleep during the daytime, they'll need a cozy, dark place to rest their eyes. Make them a pouch out of felt. This fabric is safe, since it won't unravel and get stuck on their nails.

A suggie nibbles on a mealworm—a treat that can be part of a healthy diet. To eat, sugar gliders pick up their food with their front paws.

Chapter Four

TENDER LOVING CARE

Suggie owners say they spend one to two hours a day taking care of their pets both in playtime and for food preparation.

When you let your sugar glider out of its cage, you need to make sure your house is pet proof. All of the toilet lids in your house must be closed. Sugar gliders can't swim—if they fall in, they'll drown. You'll also want to make sure that your sinks have stoppers to cover the drains. In the wild, sugar gliders live inside holes in trees. If they see a hole in your sink, they might crawl down inside and get trapped. Sugar gliders also like to climb behind refrigerators, ovens, and dishwashers. It's probably best to keep them out of the kitchen and bathroom altogether. In fact, you may want to let your sugar glider play in only one room of the house. That way you can better control what it does out of its cage.

For safety, never take your sugar glider outside. It can hop off your shoulder and disappear in the nearest tree. Or another animal might jump up and try to harm it. You should never put your sugar glider on a leash. Leashes can harm the skin on its neck and tear the patagium that lets it glide.

Sugar gliders have a very strict diet. They must eat the right kinds of food or they will get very sick. One of the main causes of death in pet sugar gliders is a poor diet. Suggies need to have a diet that is 25 percent fruit, 25 percent vegetables, and 50 percent

Feed your pet sugar glider the same types of foods it would eat in the wild. Gliders must eat fresh fruits, vegetables, and protein in order to stay healthy. Be sure to discuss your sugar glider's diet with a breeder or your vet.

Food Suggestions for Sugar Gliders

Protein	Fruits	Vegetables
shrimp	grapes (cut in half)	green beans
chicken	blueberries	corn (cut raw off the cob)
cooked eggs	apples	tomatoes
mealworms	melon	kale
feeder mice		potatoes

protein (PROH-teen). Pet food companies do not make special sugar glider food (like cat food or dog food) that is sold in stores. You have to prepare food for your glider yourself—and this takes a lot of time. It can also be quite expensive. You should plan on spending at least $50 per month on food for one sugar glider. Suggies like to eat leafy green vegetables, berries, tropical fruits, and insects. You can also add treats and biscuits to their diet, but you shouldn't do this very often. All food needs to be cut into bite-size chunks so that they can grab it with their tiny paws.

Sugar gliders also like to eat yogurt and flowers such as snapdragons, lilac, dandelions, baby's breath, and hibiscus. Never feed your suggie chocolate, caffeine, butter (even eggs cooked in butter), processed sugar, marshmallows, salt, bread, or candy.

Sugar gliders learn from their parents how to **groom** themselves. They can keep themselves clean, but it's your responsibility to keep their cages clean. Sugar gliders are quite messy. Usually, anything within

"If I lick here, I get water." Fresh water is just as important for suggies as it is for you. Make sure you check your pet's water bottle every day.

two feet of their cage is going to be splattered with food and animal waste. Every morning, you should pick up any old food from the cage and bowls. Make sure your pets have clean, fresh water. Every couple of days, you'll also have to completely clean the cage. If you allow your animal to live in filthy surroundings, it will get ill. Some suggies will actually chew on themselves when they are sick. If your suggie does this, take it to a **vet** right away.

Sugar gliders also need their toenails clipped regularly. They don't like to have this done, so you'll need to ask someone to hold the animal while you clip the nails. Or you could take your suggie to the vet, and people there will clip them for you.

It's important to take your pet to the vet at least once a year for a checkup. Research your area to find a vet who specializes in **exotic** pets. A vet who mainly

Suggies love to play and hide. They will mark their toys and beds with their scent. Once your suggie gets to know you, it will mark you as a friend, too.

works with cats and dogs will probably not have the knowledge necessary for taking care of your suggie.

When you first get your sugar glider, it might be a little afraid of you. To help your pet bond with you, let it get used to your scent. You can do this in two ways. First, while its sleeping in its felt bed, put the bed in your shirt pocket. Second, when the sugar glider is playing in its cage, drape some of your worn clothes over the top. When your sugar glider is used to how you smell, it will soon know you are its friend.

When handling your sugar glider, always pick it up from in front and underneath, with your other hand over its back. Don't hold it too tightly or it might get scared and bite you. Just let the sugar glider climb freely on you—like you are the branches of a tree—and everything will be all right.

Suggies hardly weigh anything at all. Even as adults, they are lightweight enough to ride inside the pocket of your shirt.

THE GOOD, THE BAD, AND THE UGLY

Are you still thinking that you want a pet sugar glider? Remember, they can live for up to 15 years. If you get a suggie when you're 8 years old, it could still be climbing in its cage when you're 23, which means you might have to take it to college with you. That might sound great, but some people may not want to take care of a pet for that long.

Also remember that sugar gliders are fairly messy. They tend to spray juices and toss food around when they eat. You'll always have to be cleaning up after your pet. Sugar gliders also cannot be toilet trained. They will **urinate** all over their cage—and on you when you hold them. They can't control when and where they drop their **feces**.

Sugar gliders need a lot of attention. If they don't play with you every day, they can get lonely and sad. This can make them sick, and they might even die from it. It's best if they have a fellow suggie to play with, but they'll also have to spend hours playing with you. Instead of playing outside with your friends after school, you'll have to play with your sugar glider every night. On the other hand, the kids at school might think your pet is so cool that they'll come to your house to see it. Having a sugar glider as a pet can be a great way to make friends.

Sugar gliders have a slight odor. To keep the smell down, keep their cage clean and make sure you feed them the right foods. Too many treats can cause your sugar glider to smell funny. Don't use cedar shavings in the bottom of the cage. Wood tends to hold in the sugar glider's odor more than other types of bedding.

If you have a sugar glider, you probably can't have other types of pets. Sugar gliders will bite to try to protect themselves from larger animals. They also can be dangerous to smaller animals like birds and mice. If you already have pets or want other ones, it isn't a good idea to get a suggie.

Sugar gliders are also not the best pets for small children. They have sharp claws and teeth and will scratch and sometimes bite. They also make lots of noise. At night when it's really quiet, your family might have trouble sleeping if your pet is barking, crabbing, and hissing.

Before you make up your mind, you should visit a person who has a sugar glider. See what it's really like

Gliders might look fun as ear muffs, but they should only be "worn" this way inside. Never take your sugar gliders outside. They could get hurt.

to have one as a pet. Find out how much work it will actually take to care for suggies.

Another thing you must do is find out if it is legal to have sugar gliders in your area. Some states have outlawed the pets because these animals are not native to the United States. Call your local fish and wildlife office to find out.

Once you've thought about the good and bad things about owning sugar gliders, you may decide that this pet is not for you. That's okay. There are many other types of pets that may be a better match for you.

If you decide that this pet is for you, you must convince your parents that you can care for one. The best way to do this is to explain all the drawbacks about the animal first, then tell them how you will tackle those issues. For example, your parents probably don't want to have food, urine, and feces all

Just like other animals, gliders make noises that are unique to them. This suggie seems to be singing a song. Wouldn't it be fun to know what it was saying?

over their living room carpet. Tell them you will keep your pet in one room only. Although you might be tempted to keep your suggie in the garage, this is not a good idea. Suggies need to stay in a room at a constant temperature. And they need your company.

If your parents are concerned with how much it will cost to take care of the pet, you can offer to help pay for it. Maybe you could do extra chores around the house. You could also offer to stop going to the movies and other places with your friends to help save money.

In the end, if your parents say no, you must respect their decision. You might have to wait until you are a grown-up to get one of these pets. In the meantime, you can visit sugar gliders in pet stores or at the zoo. Or you can make friends with someone who has a suggie, and you can go over and play with it as often as he or she will allow.

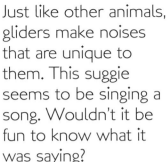

Books and Articles

Benzinane, Shana. *Rainforest Friends: Sugar Gliders.* New York: Scholastic, 2006.

Brewer, Peggy. *Sugar Gliders: Living With and Caring For Sugar Gliders: Is this the Right Pet for You?* Bloomington, Indiana: Authorhouse, 2007.

Works Consulted

Blakeley, Kiri. "Forget Fido." *Forbes.* August 7, 2000. Vol. 166. Issue 4, p. 152.

Duffield, K.S. "Sugar Gliders." *Boys' Quest.* Oct/Nov 2000. Vol. 6 Issue 3, p. 10.

Feldman, Ruth Tenzer. "Animal Angles." *Odyssey.* May 2007. Vol. 16, Issue 5, pp. 48–49.

"Gliding into the Market." *Alberta Report/Newsmagazine.* August 28, 1995. Vol. 22, Issue 37, p. 27.

"Koala Cousins." *Ranger Rick.* December 1, 1995.

"Man's New Best Friend." *Alberta Report/Newsmagazine.* July 8, 1996. Vol. 23, Issue 20, p. 21.

"Pocket Planes." *U.S. Kids.* Oct/Nov 1999. Vol. 12, Issue 7, p. 19.

Reeves, Terri D. "Cuddly Marsupial Glides into Hearts of Loving Owners." *St. Petersburg Times.* April 3, 2000.

Rindge, Brenda. "Pet Helpers Seeking Owners for Sugar Gliders." *The Post and Courier.* March 8, 2005.

Siegel, Ann Cameron. "Light as Air." *Washington Post.* July 12, 2004.

FIND OUT MORE

"Sugar Glider Fun Facts." http://www.drsfostersmith.com/
    pic/article.cfm?articleid=799
"Sugar Gliders." http://www.seaworld.org/Animal-
    info/animal-bytes/animalia/eumetazoa/coelomates/
    deuterostomes/chordata/craniata/mammalia/
    diprotodontia/sugar-glider.htm

Web Addresses
Glider Central
    http://www.glidercentral.net/
International Sugar Glider Association
    http://www.isga.org/home.htm
Sugar Glider Authority
    http://sugargliderauthority.com/
Sugar Gliders and Gliderpedia
    http://www.sugarglider.com

Rescues
Sugar Glider Rescue Railroad
    http://www.sugar-glider-rescue-railroad.org/
Suggie Savers
    http://suggiesavers.org/index.html
Worldwide Sugar Glider Network
    http://worldwidesugarglidernetwork.com/

GLOSSARY

chinchilla (chin-CHIL-ah)—A squirrel-sized rodent that is native to South America.

eucalyptus (yoo-kuh-LIP-tus)—A tall tree that is native to Australia.

exotic (ek-ZAH-tik)—From another part of the world.

feces (FEE-sees)—Solid bodily waste.

groom—To keep (a body) clean and neat.

marsupial (mar-SOO-pee-ul)—An animal that carries its young inside a pouch.

monitor (MAH-nih-tur)—A tropical meat-eating lizard that can range in size from a few centimeters to three meters long.

neutered (NOO-terd)—Made incapable of reproducing.

nocturnal (nok-TUR-nul)—Animals that are most active at night.

opossums (oh-PAH-sums)—Marsupials that are nocturnal and often hang by their tails from the branches of the trees that are their home.

patagium (puh-TAY-jee-um)—Flat, parachute-like piece of skin that is connected to a gliding animal at the wrist and ankle.

protein (PROH-teen)—A part of foods such as meats, insects, and beans that helps muscle grow.

quoll (KWOHL)—A marsupial about the size of a cat that is native to Australia.

unique (yoo-NEEK)—Unlike anything else in a category.

urinate (YUR-ih-nayt)—To release liquid bodily waste.

vet—A doctor that takes care of animals.

wombats (WOM-bats)—Marsupials, about the size of a small bear, that are native to Australia and burrow for food.

INDEX